# Nocturnes

## Poems by

### Barbara Mooney

Bloomington, IN  Milton Keynes, UK

authorHOUSE®

*AuthorHouse™*
*1663 Liberty Drive, Suite 200*
*Bloomington, IN 47403*
*www.authorhouse.com*
*Phone: 1-800-839-8640*

*AuthorHouse™ UK Ltd.*
*500 Avebury Boulevard*
*Central Milton Keynes, MK9 2BE*
*www.authorhouse.co.uk*
*Phone: 08001974150*

*First published by AuthorHouse 6/26/2007*

*ISBN: 978-1-4259-8989-7 (sc)*

*Printed in the United States of America*
*Bloomington, Indiana*

*This book is printed on acid-free paper.*

This book is dedicated to my husband Robert

# Acknowledgements

I remain in happy debt to the Live Poets Society of Boca Grande for their constructive criticism and encouragement.

My gratitude surrounds Mariela Camara for her helpful suggestions and her interpretation of my blind script.

# Table of Contents

# Of Light

Each morning I wake to incandescence.
Light has traveled ninety-three million miles
to wrap me in its solar net.

I am small prey but the net
is swift enough to capture
the osprey's ravenous plunge,
the cheetah at hunting stride upon the Serengeti
and wide enough to catch our hurtling globe.

And this net is fine and strong
as the web of a spider.
It can entrap the beginnings of a smile
or harvest the bubbles of laughter.

Yes, each morning I open the window
to become a fortunate prisoner of sun.

# A Romantic View

Daily in crowded streets,
our language ebbs,
reduced to the old harsh words.
Daily the airwaves rasp
in the brutal accents of pornography.
Abandon this dull scene.
Let us explore the mystery of desire.

Return now to the earliest of orchards.
Ignore that sex-starved snake
with his temptations.  It was young Eve
lured Adam with her apple breasts.

Or move beyond the metaphor of myth.
Let us explore the history of passion.
Recall that fabulous kidnapping
when Bothwell rode uphill through heather,
through the darkening woods, to the castle keep.
How that impetuous Earl leaned down
to swing a red-haired Queen
across his amorous saddle.

Or speak to me of young Victoria;
how a German princeling kneeled
to kiss her imperious hand
with his warm lips, how his soft gold beard
feathered against her pulse
and sent shock waves to her virginal heart.

Or thrust me back a few millenniums
to that peerless city-state
when we stood, timeless, on a pillared porch,
our marble feet at rest upon the stones,
our marble arms outstretched in a white welcoming
when you were Pericles and I, Aspasia.

# 8 A.M.

It is morning.
While the coffee perks
I turn on TV.
Into my lap, disaster pours,
earthquakes in Turkey, in China,
the freight of bone
from Iraq, from Palestine.
On the Ohio interstate
a madman sights his rifle.
The goose-steps echo
in North Korea.
Plutonium is for barter.

Mr. Coffee whispers.
I leap up.
From my lap outrage cascades
onto the floor, shattering.

I sit by the kitchen window.
The bougainvillea is content
to climb the porch.
At the pond's edge,
stands my sentinel,
a great blue heron
steeped in stillness.
Our planet sun caresses
his bright image in the water.
Two brown ducks swim
side by side through gold.
Nine ducklings, count them,
venture into light.
I lift my cup.
Briefly I am in jeopardy of joy.

## A Few Questions

What will we do when the ice is gone?
Where will the Telluride sled dogs run?
Martinis will warm in the westering sun
when the Arctic melts.
When the waters rise. What cities to save?
The time is short, the question grave.
Who will witness La Tour Eiffel
collapsing into a tidal swell
while the greening acres of
Central Park become the home
of the hammerhead shark
when Antarctica melts.

# Mother's Day

It is early morning.
I am in bed with my son.
He is nine days old.
He has dined well, lies limp
in the languor of satisfied greed.
His petalled skin is smooth
as the new tulips outside my window.
His eyelashes sprout daily, too.
His fists are curled,
the thumbs tucked safe inside
still clinging to the Darwinian branch.

I hear footsteps.
It is my husband bearing
a propitiatory cup,
steaming ambrosia.
He's a nice man.
He likes women.
Women like him.
They like his Irishness,
the bronze glints in his hair,
his pale eyes, blue-grey
like the horizon on a rainy day,
the embrace of his smile.
He makes excellent coffee.
The door opens.
I close my eyes, feigning sleep,
for on the pillow next to me
lingers a love so large
I can accommodate no other.

## In time of war:
## Pavane for my children at bedtime

On feathers, the night
descends to sing
dark aviaries in your room.
I stand at doorways, listening
to sparrows quarrel, the sonic boom
of geese in flight.

Old clowns shape
their pelican way
across the castled sand which spills
on sheets.  Gulls rise to play
with toys of air, white bills
agape.

Helpless, I walk
the corridor outside,
taut to a history
of birds, a voice that rides
on wider wings:  the raptor cry
of hawks, of hawks.

# The Colors of April

It's spring again
when that sweet reckoning
of life governs our orbit.
Under past snows
lie buried the lost causes,
the assassinations of
the body, of the spirit,
that stalk humanity.

It's spring again
and the greening of new courage.
Now the dog-tooth violet
braves its white way
through the decay
of last year's leaves
to ornament our path.

It's spring again.
Ride further north to watch
the furry seal-pups gather,
terrified, along the rocky coast,
yet, valiant in their soft
brown coats, prepared to launch
themselves into an unknown sea.

It's spring again.
Now, wing it south
to a warmer cape,
to link our beings
with those silver astronauts,
who wear their peril
as a badge of honor,
to inhabit with them
the glory of our small blue planet,
because it's spring again.
It's spring again.
It's spring.

# Henley Regatta, 1939

Between the Wars
the butterfly girls
descend from Daimlers.
Their summer skirts
flutter like wings
over the grassy lawns
that hem the river.

In the Stewards Enclosure
the Old Blues smile
raise Pimm's Cup
to these, their daughters
or the lovers of their sons,
young men who kneel
in the dark cavern
of the tent
ready to shoulder
their long sleek shells
toward the waiting river.

Upstream, the first eights
quiver for the race.
Now the starter
raises his pistol
fires, shouts "Go! Go!"

continued......

Downstream the Old Blues
stiffen to the shot,
tense to the command
and hurl themselves
up from the stench
of trenches to stumble
across the shell-shocked earth,
to hear the stutter
of the machine guns,
to fling themselves
into the gullies
dug by the thundering
cannons, to crouch over
the maimed bodies
of the first assault,
to shout "Stretcher-bearer"!
"Stretcher-bearer"!

Now, the Old Blues
hear other shouts
and they return
to see the Chiltern Hills,
the imperial blue sky,
the racing shells
on the River Thames.
And as they watch
the oarsmen, striving,
they feel their old hearts
thrust new blood into
the corridors
of their being,
and sense again
the primacy of young muscle
the once whippet leanness
under the jackets
bearing their college colors
and their cathedral voices rise
"Row, Trinity, Row, Jesus,
Row! Row! Row!"

# Little Song for the Neversink

No doubt!
A bout with a trout
stirs the answering sea
in our blood.
We started as swimmers
and here in our net
the jet-set of ourselves
twists his olive and gold.
Bold the fisher to deny this kin,
this capture of image begun,
these links of all things
on May mornings,
mid-stream, in rapt sun.

## Christmas Eve
## at Boca Grande, 2001

Tonight
the sea bears treasure.
Three porpoises arc
above the Gulf:
Their jubilant tails
splash silver on each tide.

Tonight
on shore, the Indian hawthorn
glows, to bind our island
with a silver ribbon
as present to the moon.

# Remembering Fred Astaire

From his thin, small-boned frame,
joy explodes.  He is strung tight
as an Amati, tuned as precise
as that connoisseur's violin.

We are not witness to the long hours
at the ballet bar, nor to the
multiple strains of exercise
that bare the construct
of his artistry.  Veiled from us
is the tedium of repetition
down that cascade of stairs
to take full measure of each dance floor.

Now, mesmerized by memory,
we look up at night
to seek the flare of that white tie,
the glint of patent leather shoes
that bridge the clouds,
those black tails in flight like wings.

Abrupt, he halts, poised and still,
teasing our expectancy.  Turning
he smiles at us, bows, and settles
the elegance of his top hat
on a moonbeam descending
to our out-stretched arms.
Then he turns, raises his silver-headed cane,
twirls forward to tap his eloquent feet
across the endless ballroom of the universe.

# Merlin

When I saw you first
the light was too bright
for seeing.
The arc sprang,
burst too close to target.
I did not see
your peaked hat
and the long, blue robe.

And so I did not witness
my own change:
how the warm, white arms
became ebony,
how the black sinews,
deltoid, pulled my own,
how Africa hung
incontinent and bitter
in the high vault
of the heart.

continued......

The wand in magic hands
unseen,
I pitched headlong
down the stairs
to a witless age.
My teeth smiled
in a glass of saline
on the bedside table.
Words flocked at the sill
of my mute tongue,
searching an exit.
The vocabulary of my eyes
sank back, speechless,
in sockets.
The sheets, drawn smooth,
tucked in,
explained this dying.

Blind, idiot, alien, old,
I lie on the pasture bed
under the summer
of your starry cloak
grown green again,
the thighs leafing
and the fingers curled,
Darwinian reflex,
over the original bough,
transformed, not knowing
without you, Wizard
I could not
be others.

# The Angler

April has twisted my wrist once again.
So I open my winter closet
and put on my fishing vest
and sling my boots over my shoulder
and hook the net to the belt on my waist
and seize my rod case
and run pell-mell down the hill
to my sofa of green moss
on the bank of the river.

There I'll assemble my rod
three ounces of tapered bamboo almost my age
culled seventy years ago
from the forest of China.
Then I'll affix the lightweight reel
I found and purchased years ago at Hardy's
that mecca for anglers
on the small narrow street
in back of St. James's Palace.
Then I will coat the tapered line with mucelin
so that it will run straight and true through the guides
and I'll tie on a nine and one-half foot leader
tapered too to a hair's breadth and I'll open my fly-box.

There nestle my treasures in their small compartments
as snug and as deadly as bees in a hive,
the Parmachene Belle, the Fan-wing Coachman
and the Wulff Coachman, but these are August flies
and the Black Gnat with a size twenty-two hook
that is hard to set
and the Dusty Miller and the Rat-Faced MacDougall
with its body of caribou hair
that floats high and dry in the swiftest current.
But I think I'll try matching the hatch
and tie on a Light Cahill.

continued......

Then I'll put on my hip boots
with their felt soles that prevent a slip
on the stream-polished stones
and I'll step into the fabled waters of the Catskills
with their old Dutch and Indian names
the upper reaches of the Beaverkill,
the Willowemoc, the West Branch of the Neversink.
But I will not turn down-stream
to cast a wet fly into Otter Pool
where the big Browns hover
under their Devonian ledges
ready to devour kith and kin.
Cannibals, cannibals all!
No, I will head up-stream
to seek out Salma Fontinalis
who swam in these waters
before man set foot on this continent.

Catch and release!  Catch and release!
But as I am about to leave
such a fine little fellow comes to my net
in his dress coat of the darkest silvered blue green,
well buttoned with handsome speckles
and wearing a bright pink cummerbund
with the slash of white cuffs on his fins
that are the badges of his identity,
and him I will keep
for I, too, am a cannibal
and a Brook trout for breakfast
is one of the glories of opening day.

# An Astral Probe

Our universe is like a naughty child.
It sulks in the black holes of outer space,
then swaggers out to hurl
new constellations into orbit.
It's in denial, refuses to accept
its slow conception in our intellect.

It puts on tantrums,
stamps old planets into stellar dust.
At last, it rips its new pajamas
into threads that float across the sky
to tantalize us with theories about strings.
Now, out of breath, it may return
to rest on the soft hemispheres of our brain
and, pillowed, fall asleep.

# Green Thumbs

I am a gardener.  I like dirt.
I like to crumble its brown essence
between my hands, ungloved.
I like to put on my frayed blue shirt
laundered fifty times to rest
like a petal against my skin.
Yes, I did wear gloves two years ago
when with my shovel I bucked in manure from
the cows in the upper pasture,
returning grass to grass.

So now I lace green cord
around my peony stems, tight corsets
to display their opulent white breasts
like so many ladies of the Imperial court.
And I will stake blue towers
of delphinium against the fence.
And I will dead-head the purple
bonnets of the iris.

Then, pride pulsing
at my handiwork, I'll turn
to stride free on our stony country road.
There in that impoverished soil
stripped bare by winter plows,
rise a bravery of daises,
and great clumps of pearly everlasting
that never wilt in my bouquets
and a Niagara fall of blackberry vines.
Beyond this display, a slope of gabions,
cages of stone-filled wire,
anchors the bank against descent.
And through these cages, rise
long green stems
topped with white umbels
which spread a haze of lace
above their prison.  I lean forward,
and admonished by a master gardener,
I kneel, penitent, before
the myriad florets that crown
the glory of Fool's Parsley.

# For Men Only

Listen, poet, statementsman.
Turn up that hearing aid.
I'm no lady.
I don't have time
to be politic.
I'll shout outside
while you balance the world
on the end of a pencil,
lecture the typewriter,
give your kind of birth.
I don't have time
for fine print, signators.
I'm tired of treaties.

Attend, all drummers,
I don't have time.
I don't have time
for your rocket'n roll,
old hat, gone, done,
danced last year.
I don't have time
for your probes to Mars.
I've heard that march before
and it's local.
I'm rocking to
a newer rhythm.

continued......

Hear me, dreamers,
I don't have time,
while you say, peering
down from the outer space
of your consciousness,
"Let's secede, darling,"
while you say
on the high balcony
of your manhood,
drawing the blinds,
"Who was that,
in that mob, out there?"

Dearest Sirs: that's us,
all that grey hair,
dyed, wigged, 14 carat,
all those rainbow thighs,
black, yellow, brown, white,
all those shapes,
slack, firm, old, young.
We're tired of accommodations.
That's us, outside,
all you poets,
all you statesmen.
We don't have time
for your four-letter words,
eden, love, hope,
to lasso creation,
because we've held it
in its crumpled,
undiapered self,
brand-new,
and its bones are basalt.
Respectfully, we've had it,
Ungentle men,
It's ours,
rock bottom.

# At The Museum

I detest pink, but then I met
this Manet girl, on loan I think
to that old robber baron, Met,
who hoards each treasure he can get.

Ensconced in her café,
winked at by passing boulevardier,
pink lips, pink arms, pink breasts now rule
over pink waterfalls of tulle.

Before her, in a crystal dish,
the sexiest plum that one could wish,
a princely purple in pink liqueur
the amorous chef has poured for her.

Enveloped in a rosy haze,
I rest my chin in hand and gaze,
knowing I totter on the brink
of love, in love with carnal pink.

# Pausing in Padova

Cappella degli Scrovegni!
There I fell prey to Giotto's blue
that stabbed the heretic heart in me.

Blue sky above the shepherd's field.
Blue the robes the Magi wore
as they knelt by the stable door.
That incandescent faith!

Stretched stunned upon the chapel stones,
I know his heaven will pick my bones
and haunt the heretic heart in me
as I lie felled by Giotto's blue.
Cappella degli Scrovegni!

# On Flight

Watching my downy sons
in their first flutter of flights,
I dwell on birds.
O, not on mother images of wrens
nor the rose-breasted finch whose words
make winter loud and long
with perched complaints.
I know of these.

Now, cresting feathers rise along my skull,
swift secondaries challenge trees
to pull the urgent sky under my vanes.
These downy sons will leave
like me, their pileate victory
on the bark.  Rise, rare,
above green leaves
and change their plumage
in full flight.

Become as I become,
not gentled wren, sage,
myna, pelican clown, but stun
the sonic sky,  accipiter,
will pulse with hunger-marks as I do now,
the harrier's curse bared
on their wings where my wings flow
until they ride utopias
of air, sweeping the warrior eye
down-forest to search
the emerald dove, the fern,
the greening prey
spread-winged on grass.  Like me
slant down the plumy cloud to stalk,
scaled talons hectoring the air.  Be
in the laurelling of my second self,
the rapturous hawk.

# In Harm's Way

There is a simple beauty
to a gun.
Take the Beretta,
sleek upon the palm
as an Italian glove
accurate short-range
to wreck the heart
of a deceiving love.
When all is said
and all is done
there is a simple beauty
to a gun.

There is a fatal beauty
to a gun.
Test the teutonic Luger
an engineering marvel in design,
dead accurate long-range
to interrupt the peace
along the Rhein.
When all is said
and all is done
there is a fatal beauty
to a gun.

continued......

There is a stunning beauty
to a gun.
From Hartford, Sam Colt
fired West to decorate
each cowboy's flank
while George S. Patton
pulling rank
had his two pistols
cased in ivory.
When all is said
and all is done
there is a stunning beauty
to a gun.

There is a deathly beauty
to a gun.
Assemble the Kalishnikov
inaccurate but so wide-spread
it carves new paths
on Russian plains
where past invaders bled.
When all is said
and nothing done
there is a deathly beauty
to a gun.

## Christmas Eve
## at Boca Grande, 2002

Tonight
the world's at dance.
Sandpipers foxtrot on the beach;
The bougainvillea tangos on its branch,
acacias shake, old rhumbas
through their leaves.

Tonight
these rhythmic steps ascend
toward the vast ballroom
of the Milky Way
to join great planets
in their waltz of joy.

# Time to Bloom

I like the size of Spring.
Try it on a bare branch.
It fits.
Pull it over a tulip's head.
It fits.
Button it high as your heart.
It fits.
Yes, this solar elastic's
quite an invention.

## Of Conflict

When war rides again
heavy on the shoulders
of the world,
the weight of bones
in that battered rucksack
is a freight
we are too old to bear.

We bend to carry lesser casualties:
a feather, fallen,
that slow kiss, remembered,
the autumn deaths of daffodils
impatient for spring.

# Acceleration

Speed, speed, we are
dead-set on speed.
Like empty cans of Coors,
the bodies line the interstate,
straddle the median,
huddle in gullies.
And why not speed? Our
very world orbits our planet
Sun in a single year.  And
planet Sun clutching
its solar satellites is tucked,
a stellar package, under the
elbow of the Milky Way as
this, our constellation, hurls
its weight in pursuit of Andromeda,
collision prone.

Speed, speed, that urgent
need swarms in our blood,
drives the beat of the heart,
mounts the double helix
of our disorderly selves,
as we fall in love
with Bravo, Bronco, Cavalier
the shape of Thunderbird.

The confection of foreign
names lies sweet upon our lips,
Isotta-Fraschini, Bugatti,
Porsche, Mercedes Benz
accelerates our bugle-blood,
for speed, speed, speed,
dead-set on speed.

# Anchor Ice

Come north with me old love.
Come north with me
and leave the sommolence
of sand, of sea,
that binds us in captivity.

Come north again, old love with me,
to plunge our aging selves
in drifts of snow,
each fabulous flake hexagonal
by architects we cannot know.

Grown weighty in our winter white
we'll thunder down to avalanche
ourselves into a stream
before our frailties
dissipate in this new cold.
We'll sink to find an anchor stone
that welds our shapes in diamond ice.
There, bright in our antiquity
we'll hold.

# The Giants

When they lift the tarps, our afternoons
ring bronze on the grassy shield
and sixty thousand throats exhale
chilled joy.  The heralds yield
their mikes to balding Lancelot.
His helmet scowls, ferocious, in his arm.
From the battered mouth, his name cavorts,
old war-horse in the sweet, warm
gaze of cameras.  He knows the game
and spikes anticipation with his cleats.
We lean, too, impaled on cold spears
of breath, rise from our seats
as one vast Guinevere and sigh.
The Grail is visible and hangs
upstairs, lace to the sun
for the brief life of kick-off.
The armies' impact huddles
in our spine.  Our maiden hair
stands upright for the prize.
Arthur, unplumed, lies buried under cheers.
We lust again, throw gages down
the ranks.  Our lava hearts spill hot
and chivalrous.  We know necessity
wars in our blood.  We are not
fanged for virtue, but for triumph,
and this arena's bigger than the world,
contained and possible.  We shudder
for mortality, nip bourbon,
clap our tourneyed souls together
in praise of them, these beautiful,
scarred men who mimic for us.
O Lancelot! O Hays! O Tarkenton!

# Let's dance

Tonight old bio-rhythms
are in charge.
The bougainvillea tangos
in the dark.
In the lagoon the river otter
sports his sinuosity.
On beach, sand-pipers
fox-trot with the waves.

Tonight
the moon-pulled tide
cavorts with the reflection
of the stars.
On shore we breathe
the sea-borne air, grow salt
and plunge our bodies
water-ward
into seines of
phosphorous and
lift our golden arms
to strum the dance.

# The Frantic Phone

Emergency Medical Service, here.
Oh, Doctor, I feel death is near.

Describe your symptoms while alive,
by pressing button number 5.

Help me. I don't think I can wait.
Do not succumb. Try number 8.

I cannot breathe. I'm on the floor.
Ah, pulmonary! Number 4.

I'm tranquil now. My life is through.
Resuscitation's number 2.

As we prepare your wings for Heaven,
to exit, please press number 7.

# Christmas Eve
# at Boca Grande, 2003

Tonight
The Gulf is calm.
The moon descends to swim
and turns small fish to silver
to ornament each tide.

Tonight
On shore, hibiscus
hushes trumpet vine.
The aerial osprey
folds his wings.
The island waits in petaled sleep
for the harmonies of dawn.

# For R., born on Memorial Day 1920

In May, good things speak out.
Peonies shout white.
All day, the wisteria blues
throb to an audience of bees,
honey-drunk,
heady as Bourbon Street.
Clamped in the border's orchestra
from their bronze and copper throats
roar anthems of iris.
Oh cacophonous garden!
What joyous noise
to celebrate your day.

# In The Orchard

I lift my granddaughter into the apple tree.
She grafts small legs about a branch
twelve times her age.
Then plummets, head down, laughing,
to orbit the original trapeze.

Eve booster by nature and my heritage,
have I made her swing too far?
What farmer Adam will mount his ladder
to pluck her smile, caress the skin
smooth as the peel of an apple,
pull the brown stem of her pony tail,
store her in the cold vault of his desire
for long keeping?

So, now, while the serpent coils,
implacable, under my heel,
now is the time to tumble her,
dearest girl, into my out-stretched arms
to hold for one morning moment,
ah, brief mourning moment,
before that final fall.

# Midsummer

The hue of love is green.
Come, let us lie
on old Utopias of grass;
mark out the sky's
blue intellect,
the pilings of the trees
where the wind docks
and warblers, too, make
ports of call
while the mind bobs
its buoy in the air,
signaling vast directions
everywhere.

So, stronger feel, under us
the commanding earth;
how Gulliver's bonds re-pin us;
how, from incandescence,
the rock flows up and pours
along our spine.
Our bones are basalt
and our structures lie
immemorial in the chilling air
waiting the green assault
that makes us beautiful,
the hue and cry of grass.

# Decades

Age 10, my husband loved to dance.
Product of a then rare divorce,
he was the first to glide
his patent leather pumps across
the ballroom floor toward
the anticipatory line of little girls,
still shy but beckoning.

Age 20, my husband loved to dance.
Secure in his hard-won scholarship,
he swept Veronica through Harvard Yard.
He twisted Pamela down Boylston Street.
His long legs carried Elizabeth up Beacon Hill.

Age 30, my husband loved to dance.
Laid in storage, were the shellings
on the Burma Road, the release of prisoner skeletons,
as he danced me past the lion's cage
in Central Park to circle the cement lagoon
that harbored a courtesy ballet of seals.

Age 40, my husband loved to dance.
We shook free of his conference in Brazil
in time to join the tribal throngs of Carnaval,
all races, all shapes, all colors, samba-ing.

continued......

Age 50, my husband loved to dance.
Weary of our stately pavane
around the Place Vendome,
we fled across the old Pont Neuf
to tango on la Rue du Chat Qui Peche.

Age 60, my husband loved to dance.
We waltzed along the great Ring Strasse
where the swastikas once hung on long
red banners stamped with the symbols
of the Hakenkreuz, the crooked cross.
Our urgent feet danced past the legacy
of war to honor Johann Strauss.

Age 70, my husband loved to dance.
At balls in Boca Grande, we watched
the fascinating young in their gyrations
who did not know we flowed across the floor,
as easy as the Ohio to the Mississippi
on that long voyage to the sea.

Age 80, my husband loved to dance.
I kneel beside his wheel-chair
to put my arms around paralysis.
"We were good dancers once",
he says in his now murmurous voice.
His blue eyes brim with laughter.
"No. Make that we were great dancers. Weren't we?"
"We are." I answer him. "Indeed, we are."

# A Recipe

I welcome all warriors into my kitchen.
Here they can behead the stems from carrots.
Here they can roast a reluctant leg of lamb.
Here, tribal chiefs can peel
the obdurate skins from old potatoes.
Here statesmen at war can whip
offending egg whites into shape.
Here they can rend importunate lettuce leaves
for the imperial Caesar's salad.
And now, aggression spent, we'll all
sit down to dine in peace together.

# The New Centurion

I am no Roman.  This harness is tougher
than Italian leather, frets more,
pinches the armpits.  I wear
the age of our constriction no better
than any other warrior.

And yet, man is more singular than men
in spite of all communal militants,
Caesar, Christ, or that old Rabbi-in-reverse
covering foolscap in the Reading Room
of a London library.

But who denies his weight?
Airborne, knees locked,
the soul in tuck position,
I feel the gravity of my age,
the downward pull.
Each atom in the escaping self
seeks splash-down.

continued......

A nuclear world now manacles my feet
and I sprawl, gasping, on my back
the harness clattered and askew.
I think, waiting for my heart
to calm its stride,
of lonely, aerial things,
of Da Vinci's final years,
how he labored for the King of France,
not with painting,
not with the cryptic script
of our mirror world,
but with fireworks:
how the mathematics of the universe
flared in a pinwheel,
how that genius was spent for the short
splendor of a rocket to amaze the Court,
the self afire in the great black night
above the forests of Fontainebleau,
consumed, consumed.

# Letting Go

Each year on the threshold of my mind
I conduct rummage sales.
Here is the mud-spattered
velvet cloak Sir Walter
flung before his Queen
to save her silken slippers
from ordure in a London street.
Yet mythic gallantry aside,
wary Elizabeth
sent her sea captain to the Tower
for coupling with her maid of honor.

And here's the long white scarf
that Isadora wound around
her throat, until the fringed ends
afloat in the wild air,
spun into the wire wheels
of the Ferrari and broke
her dancer's neck
on the curve of the Corniche
long years ago.

And here is the enormous book
embossed in long black letters, The Bible,
a tome which our diminished President,
his curls well-cropped,
held clamped to his heart
with his left hand
while with his right
he clutched the arm of his teenage daughter
as they strode across the White House lawn
to greet the ravenous Press.

And last, here's the battered
miner's lamp that will shine bright
forever, to pierce old rock-falls
in the mind and light new seams
in the bedrock of memory.

# Macular Degeneration

Large words I can
no longer read.
Honor is dimmed,
honesty veiled,
truth gone to seed.

My fingers dwell
on smaller print,
the Braille of a river's flow,
the brief kiss of
a snow flake on my pulse,
a trail of dog-tooth violets
in the woods,
that maple leaf
afire in my glove.
This small print
I love to read,
this dictionary of my world.

# A Brief Biography

Do you remember her?
Daisy Chain girl with the
dark waterfall of hair
the surprise of those eyes
blue and wide denying her beauty,
wild with intelligence.

Do you remember him?
That crazy paratrooper
his eyes as shiny
above his broken nose
as his jump boots below.
Yes, as shiny as
his sun-filled voice.

Do you remember her?
That small woman
voluptuous and fierce
as any tiger
who drove her Morris Minor
through Persia and the Khyber Pass
to Islamabad.

Do you remember him?
Cavalier, born three hundred
years too late
striding across Grand Central
in his dark blue
pinstripe disguise
his red hair afire
in the slants of sun
his arms opening.

How many young and splendid ghosts
walk the long corridors of the mind?

# In Autumn

Frost last night, and deep.
On the back porch, my garden gloves
stand upright, frozen. I run
down the hill to the garden gate,
fenced against the blight of
the raptorial deer with their great
brown eyes, their 20-20 sight,
the razor cut of their hooves,
their plundering muzzles.

I undo the latch. Oh desolate vision!
The great green leaves of the
zucchini plant crumpled, clenched tight
as the Victorian fan snapped shut in
the face of an importunate suitor. To the right,
my French lettuces, Merveille des Quatre Saisons.
Give up your title. You have lasted two seasons only,
your fringed delicacy as limp as my autumn hands.
Oh, marvel of four seasons!
No accomplished liar can match the tall tales
told by a seed catalog.

And my beans! The heroic scimitars of wax beans,
the rapier pole beans, my vegetable army all defeated
and I feel the slow ebbing of my summer blood.
I stamp my angry spade into the garden soil.
Bury the fallen while the light remains.
The handle vibrates. Now I know. I remember.
I dig with care. I pull from the treasury of its
cave the fabulous orange sword
I stand tall, waving my trophy.
I will survive November.
I'll outlast frost. I have carrot roots.

# Advisory

How do we speak to the future?
In what language,
in what parlance of understanding?
In what accents
do we suborn perjury
when we laud the tempestuous century
in which we spent our lives?

We need no knowledge of alien tongues;
not of Russian, Mandarin, Arabic, Urdu
nor of the Romantic languages, nor of
Farsi or Finno-Ugric, or Teutonic phrases.
English is in the cockpit
and rides the vapor trails
that seal our globe.

But our intent is not
the pursuit of dialect
by which to explore our history.
Perhaps we shall not burden the future
with the legends of so many,
like themselves, lost on our watch.

continued......

Perhaps, if they search new directions,
we shall tell them
to view the warblers winging north
on the Canadian flyway
or to note the armada of great hawks
as they drift the thermals south.
Perhaps we shall tell them not to envy
the jewels in the crown
when they possess a hoard of diamonds
in the anchor ice of a winter stream.

Perhaps we shall tell them
not to heed the beat
of the distant drums
but to attend to the beat
of the heart that lies so close to their own.
Perhaps, if we are wise,
they will still listen.

# The Flight of the Swallowtails

In the terminal ward
they lie cocooned in blankets
still clinging to the sturdy
branches of their hospital beds;
their heads at rest on the
white blossom of their pillow.
They are mute. They are waiting.

They do not recall the inventory,
of their lives, not the brief
stutter of childhood
nor the full fledged utterance
of ambition, nor the intimate
oratory of passion. Wrapped
in the skeins of their mortality,
they remain speechless,
waiting for the chrysalis to split open.

Ah, then they will emerge
to fan their exquisite, still-damp wings
in the evening air. Soon, they will
drift to the opening door, those wings
as yellow, as transparent
as slants of sun-light,
stitched into tapestry
by threads of black.
Now, brave in their fragility,
they will flutter out
into the vast star-studded
universe where they were born.

## Christmas Eve
## at Boca Grande, 2004

Tonight
after the wrath of hurricanes
the air grows still.
Our damaged island lies peaceful
in a tranquil sea.

Tonight
this stillness falls upon the world,
tethers the hurricanes within the heart
and quells the torment
of those wilder seas.

# Inquiry

Who birthed the wind thirteen billion years ago?
Astronomers say they know the date
but who could manhandle planets into space
without galactic winds?
Who turns our globe without the wind?

In the depths of his sailor's heart,
Columbus knew these Westerlies.
New pilots dream on jet streams in their sleep.
Who allows winds to surge the vast Pacific
from its bed?

Yesterday, happier girls slanted past me
on the bike path, their roller blades
tuned to the tarmac, their long hair fanned
in the hands of the wind.

Yes, and this morning when I rose
from our bed to open the window
the salt air, like him,
took me in its arms enraptured.
Who began the struggles of loving
thirteen billion years ago?

# Of Winter

Ah blizzard!
In the woods
all things are white,
transformed.

The black pines shoulder
epaulets of snow.
Gone is the summer
sinuosity of brown,
weasel turned ermine.

Even the red fox pokes
a silvered muzzle
from his den.

The deer in their ghost-grey
winter coats
flounder in drifts.
They will not survive.

In April we walk these woods,
the dead leaves crisping underfoot,
while above a renaissance
of green begins.

We examine the white bones
on the floor of the forest
and we think of snow-death
and the exquisite shape
of hexagons,
flakes as varied as planets,
and the blizzard
storms through our brain,
great gusts from the
perfect universe
we cannot know.

# We, Argonauts

The shore is darkening. Symposiums of gulls,
white as scholars, gather on a wave.
Underneath our stricken feet, the long hull
pulls through lingering water.

On the grave beach, the shining pebble of a child
rolls home.  Voiceless, we scan
the slow divorce of land, and further, the mild
adieus of tree-tops.

Had we a plan of conquest for that gentleness? To sail
armadas in the blood, barrack the woods with shouts,
tread pulses of grass into a road?  We fail
in the remembering.  Only our flags are out,
scarring the wind.

The D-Day weapons lie in wreaths below.
Unarmed, we are not innocent.
We breathe again the warrior sea, grow salt,
and turning, eye, nailed to the mast,
our tarnished fleece.

# Of Water

Love is the aquifer
from which we draw our joy.
It flows between the dry
arroyos of our minds
to bring new thought to leaf.

Love pours into deep
cellars to flood
old vintages of hate
until their labels
peel away, illegible.

Love is the slow river,
now the meander that gentles
our wild meadow-children
to summer harvest.

As we lie on the bedrock
of desire, love is the stream
that pulses through our
primal blood toward ardency.

Refresher of all life
love is our aquifer.

Printed in the United States
97083LV00003B/328-330/A